The Secret:
How to Fight Child Protective Services and Win

Vincent W. Davis, Attorney at Law

www.FightChildProtectiveServices.com
www.VincentWDavis.com

Copyright © 2015 Vincent W. Davis

All rights reserved.

ISBN-13: 978-1514899366
ISBN-10: 1514899361

DEDICATION

This book is dedicated to my late wife
Denise Doucette-Davis.

Without your support,
mentoring and confidence,
I would not have learned
what it really means
to help clients.

Contents

1. Introduction 11
   About the Author: 11
   Primary Purpose: 12
2. The Juvenile Dependency Court System 15
3. The Social Worker's Initial Investigation 17
4. First Court Hearing: The Arraignment & Detention Hearing (A&D) 23
5. Placement With Relatives & Family Friends 27
6. The Pre-Release Investigation (PRI) 29
7. The Jurisdictional Hearing (JDX, ROR) 31
8. The Contested Jurisdictional Hearing (ADJ, Trial #1) 35
   What Happens at the Trial 38
9. The Dispositional Hearing (Dispo, Trial #2) 41
10. The 388 Petition & Hearing 45
11. The Sixth Month Review (364, .21E, JR) 47
12. The Twelve Month Review Hearing (.21F, PPH) 55
13. The Selection & Implementation Hearing (.26) 59
    A. 388 petition (See Chapter 10) 61
    B. Bonding Study 62
    C. Notice of Appeal 62
14. Foster Parents Rights 65
15. The Secret 69

ACKNOWLEDGMENTS

I would like to acknowledge my hundreds and hundreds (probably more than a thousand) of juvenile dependency clients. Without you, this book would not have been possible.

Representing all of you has been truly a blessing. I have been helped by you through your human experiences, more than I have helped you with my legal representation.

1. Introduction

About the Author:

Vincent W. Davis is a licensed attorney in the State of California. He is the managing member of the Law Offices of Vincent W. Davis & Associates.

www.VincentWDavis.com,
www.FightChildProtectiveServices.com,
Phone: (888) 888-6582
v.davis@VincentWDavis.com

The law firm currently has two attorneys who practice primarily in the area of Juvenile Dependency law. They have represented families in the following counties, where they currently have open cases as of the writing of this book:

Los Angeles
Orange
San Bernardino
Riverside

San Diego
Ventura
San Francisco

Mr. Davis and his firm have handled more than a thousand juvenile cases over the past 25 years, where he has represented parents, family members, foster parents and even the children themselves.

He is an expert in the area of Juvenile Dependency law, and an expert trial attorney, which is attributed to his vast experience and training. He is a graduate of the prestigious Gerry Spence Trial Lawyers College; and relies heavily on the trial skills and techniques taught to him by Gerry Spence (who many consider the greatest trial lawyer in American history).

Primary Purpose:

The primary purpose of this book is to give an introduction, and only an introduction, and outline of the Juvenile Dependency Court System in California to parents and relatives involved in this court system. The details and specifics of any one particular case, or type of case, are far more complex than what can be handled in a book of this nature. Further, my 28 years as an attorney cannot be summed up in an introductory book of this type. If you have specific questions you must consult with a competent attorney. At this time, we offer free initial consultations. Call me at (888) 888-6582.

This book is also written for the purpose of assisting parents and family members in figuring out what they should be doing during this process, and what they can do to assist their attorneys. It is my strong recommendation that, if your children are ever taken by a County social worker, or if you are investigated by a County social worker, talk to an attorney FIRST! Do not assume the social worker is your friend. The worst thing that could happen is you lose custody of your children, possibly forever.

This book is intended to be informational ONLY. It is not intended to form an attorney-client relationship. Nor is it intended to give specific legal advice. For specific legal advice you should contact a competent attorney who will advise you of your rights. Or you can call me, for a free initial consultation.

(888) 888-6582.

2. The Juvenile Dependency Court System

The Juvenile Dependency Court System is administrated by two different entities. The Superior Court of California, Juvenile Dependency Departments - which is part of every County Superior Court system in California. This system is part of the judicial branch of the local government.

The County social works have different names from County to County. In Los Angeles, they are referred to as the Department of Children and Family Services (DCFS). In most parts of the state, they are referred to as Child Protective Services (CPS). These departments are part of the executive branch of the local government.

Cases generally start with an investigation by the county social workers, which could, but not always, involve the local or federal police agencies. A juvenile dependency investigation sometimes leads to a criminal investigation, which is separate and apart from the social worker's investigation. It is my advice that you DO NOT talk to a county social worker, or a policeman, without first consulting with an attorney. It could lead to you losing your children, forever, or going to jail and being convicted of crimes.

3. The Social Worker's Initial Investigation

Juvenile Dependency cases usually begin in two ways. First, the social worker, generally an Emergency Response (ER) worker, becomes aware of the suspected child abuse, which was reported by a third person. California, like most states, has a long list of "mandated reporters" of suspected child abuse. Teachers, doctors, therapists, day care providers, or any other person(s), can call ANONYMOUSLY and report suspected child abuse to a County social worker.

For example, your child attends school, and the teacher notices some sort of bodily injury to the child, or the child tells the teacher s/he has some sort of injury caused by someone in your home. The teacher must report the suspected child abuse, and the County social worker's investigation begins.

The second way cases generally start is when there is some sort of police involvement, and your children are present. For example, you are pulled over in your car for suspected driving under the influence, and your children are in the car. More than likely, the police will contact the local county social worker hotline; the social worker will come out, and take your child into custody. In this situation, you'd most likely be arrested for driving under the influence, and child endangerment, and your child will most likely be placed in a foster home or with relatives.

You'd then have two cases, a criminal and a Juvenile Dependency case.

During this process, the social worker is supposed to advise you of your right to speak to an attorney; but, this is rarely done. And it seems there is no adequate remedy for this failure. In the criminal court system, if the police don't advise you of your right to an attorney before you speak to them, your statements could be excluded from evidence.

Not so in the juvenile court system, where your comments can lead to not only losing your children, in some cases forever; but it could also lead to you being criminally prosecuted. Your statements to a social worker can be used against you in juvenile court, AND in criminal court. And in most cases, social workers are all too happy to testify against you in criminal proceedings.

So, my general advice, based on almost 28 years of experience, is - DO NOT talk to social workers without consulting an attorney! And, as you've no doubt seen on TV and the movies, don't talk to a police officer without consulting an attorney. I know this is simple advice, but I see, all too many times, where parents and relatives violate this advice, because the social worker acted as if h/she were trying to assist them, or outright intimidate them. Please don't be fooled.

Now I have to say, there are good social workers. But it's better to be safe than sorry.

Recently, a client told me that she spoke to the social worker, because the social worker said something to the effect, "If you don't talk to me, and answer my questions, it will make you look bad in front of the judge." And, this might be true, but it might not be. However, I can assure you, if you talk to the social worker, most times you are going to look bad, because you don't know the law, you don't know what you should say, nor what you shouldn't say. So the simple advice is, don't say anything - until you can speak to a lawyer.

From a lawyer's perspective, if you don't talk to the social worker h/she can't gather information and evidence against you. Most likely, the worker didn't observe how an injury occurred; so your words become the main evidence against you.

Finally, if a social worker comes to your home, you do not, I repeat you do not have to let them in your home, nor do you have to talk to them. This is America, and a Warrant or Court Order is required for them to gain access into your home. Many times, the social worker will show up at your home with the local police. The same rule applies, you do not have to talk to them, and you do not have to let them in your home, unless they have a warrant or a court order.

In some cases, the worker or police may claim an emergency situation, and demand entry into your home. At this point, it may be prudent to allow them in, but you should not speak to them. Although, they do have the right to speak with your children. If this happens, contact a lawyer immediately.

During this initial investigation, the social worker can do several things. First, the social worker can immediately initiate a court case. There is usually nothing you can do about this but go to court, and consult with an attorney.

Second, the social worker may conduct a further investigation, which may take a few days to several weeks. Again, don't talk to the worker, and do NOT sign any forms agreeing to do anything. This is a way the social worker can gather evidence against you.

Recently, we had a case in San Diego County. The social worker went to the mother's home and got the mother to agree the children would be removed from her home for 30 days (without going to court). The mother signed various forms, including to have the mother drug tested.

Then the mother called me. I immediately revoked all the releases of information, and advised the worker my client would not be drug testing. The worker informed the mother that, if she followed my advice, she'd file a case against her. The problem was that the social worker did not have enough evidence to start or win a juvenile case; unless my client did what the social worker wanted. In the end, the children were returned, and no case was filed – not enough evidence. Remember, if you talk, that will be evidence against you.

4. First Court Hearing: The Arraignment & Detention Hearing (A&D)

After your children are taken by the social worker, the law requires that you be given the opportunity to go to court and challenge the social worker. This can be a long process.

The social worker has to notify you, within 48 hours of you losing your children, that you have a court date. Some counties use the 72 hour rule, which some appellate courts have upheld, despite what the statute requires.

If you are taken to court after this time, request that your attorney make a motion to dismiss the case for failure to have your first hearing within the required time frame (the 48 hour rule). This issue could become important later.

At this first hearing, you should have hired a competent private attorney to represent you in this matter. If you did not hire an attorney, California law requires that a court-appointed attorney be given to you to represent you in this matter. Just like if there were a criminal case, if you are unable to afford an attorney, one will be appointed to represent you. First, in most counties, you will be required to pay the County back for your court-appointed attorney (s/he is not free); but, this avenue is probably less expensive than hiring your own attorney.

But like in a criminal case, serious consideration should be given to hiring a competent private attorney. A private attorney may have some advantages over a public defender. But, this decision should be made on a case by case basis.

At this initial hearing, you and your attorney will be given the "discovery" in the case. This generally includes the allegations filed against you, and the supporting documentation, including the California Welfare and Institutions Code (WIC) section 300 petition, the Application for petition, and the Detention Report.

Not all children are recommended to be removed from their parent/s.

But, in cases where this is recommended by the social worker, it is important that you and your attorney review the discovery documents, and try to craft arguments as to why the children should be returned to your custody.

The difficult thing at this hearing, and this hearing only, is that the judge must accept the allegations by the social worker as true. After this hearing, the social worker must prove the case against you.

If you are in disagreement with the judge's ruling, California law allows you to have a detention rehearing. At this rehearing, you may cross examine the social worker, live and on the stand; and in some cases, the judge may permit you to present some limited evidence on your own.

> Hint: The best way to present evidence is to use the evidence during the cross examination of the Emergency Response (ER) social worker. Otherwise, the judge may not permit you to present a "case in chief", or present separate evidence at this hearing. You may have to wait to present such evidence at the adjudication/Jurisdictional hearing at a later date.

The most important thing for you to know at this hearing is that you have a right to a speedy trial. If the children are removed from your custody, your trial may be within 15 judicial days; if the children are not removed, your trial may be within 30 judicial days.

The reason this is important is that a lot of juvenile court rooms are extremely busy, and your trial may be scheduled for a date 2 or 3 times past the 15 or 30 day limit.

Now, in some circumstances, this may be beneficial to the parents; sometimes not. But in any event, it is the sort of thing you should know, and you should consider, when scheduling your next dates at the initial hearing.

5. Placement With Relatives & Family Friends

Many times, children are placed in foster homes when they are taken from parents.

In my opinion, placement with friendly relatives is always better than placement in a foster home. The reasons for this opinion are almost infinite, but include: better visitation schedule (frequency & duration) for the parents; children are in a more familiar environment, and there is less trauma for parents and children in arranging for scheduled visitation.

6. The Pre-Release Investigation (PRI)

On occasion, the judge may set an interim hearing, if requested, for the home of a relative or parent to be investigated, so that the children can be placed there, and not in foster care.

I find that these types of hearings are being used less and less; and being asked for less and less by the defense attorneys. Technically, this type of hearing is not authorized by the letter of the law (the statutes), but I've always argued that such a hearing can be held under the court's discretionary power, especially where the spirit of the law requires children to be placed with relatives instead of foster homes. But if the occasion arises, it is always helpful for a family if the social worker is ordered to do the relative placement investigation by a certain date, with a report back to the court on a certain date.

Obviously, this can accelerate the placement of the children with family.

Problems arise when the social worker's report is disputed by the family member, then the question becomes, "will the judge allow some sort of contested hearing on this issue?"

7. The Jurisdictional Hearing (JDX, ROR)

After the Arraignment & Detention Hearing, the case is assigned to a social worker called a Dependency Investigator (DI). It is this workers job to independently, and objectively, investigate the allegations of the Emergency Response (ER) social worker, the allegations in the WIC 300 petition, including reviewing documents and interviewing witnesses.

It is my humble opinion that these investigations are not independent, nor objective in most cases. Please note, I wrote "most," not "all." However, more times than not, the Dependency Investigator supports the claims of the ER worker, because they do not want to be sued later by the family.

Is there ever child abuse committed by a parent? "Yes." But is there ever inaccurate or exaggerated reporting by the DI? "Yes."

I'm currently involved in a case where the DI seems to have copied - word for word - the

ER worker's report. And in my investigation, it seems to appear that the social worker has not talked to the witnesses independently.

Not too long ago, an ER worker wrote in her report that the child's counselor said that the child was being "emotionally abused", or words to that effect. The DI wrote in her report that very same thing, and made it seem like she had spoken with the therapist.

At the Contested Jurisdictional Hearing, I subpoenaed the therapist to testify. The therapist testified that she never told the ER worker anything about the child being emotionally abused. She further testified that she'd never met or even spoken with the DI.

The report prepared by the Dependency Investigator for this hearing usually contains proposed factual findings, as well as recommendations for the children. Essentially, the report, in this case, recommended that the court should take jurisdiction of the children, and gave conditions and recommendations. These recommendations included, where the children should reside: parent's home, relative home, or foster home. And it also recommended, if the children were not returned home, what classes and therapy the parents should participate in, in order to regain or keep custody of the children.

If the parent is not in agreement with some, or all, of the recommendations, s/he has the constitutional right to a trial. This includes the right to subpoena witnesses to testify and be cross-examined.

At this hearing, the attorney generally recommends that the client accept some sort of plea bargain to settle the case. This would usually mean that the parent would plead "no contest" to some or all of the allegations in the WIC 300 petition. I don't ever recommend a plea bargain, unless there is some sort of advantage to my client. And, if there is no plea bargain, there must be a trial.

8. The Contested Jurisdictional Hearing (ADJ, Trial #1)

Assuming that you were not in agreement with some or all of the recommendations of the DI in the Jurisdictional/Dispositional report filed by the social worker; you are entitled to a trial. I refer to this trial as the Adjudication Hearing, or trial number 1 (ADJ, Trial#1).

The first thing you should do is schedule a meeting with your attorney to review and develop a legal strategy that could lead to the return of the children to your home.

Important things have to be completed for trial preparation:

    a. The interview of certain witnesses, if possible

    b. The subpoenaing of these witnesses to court, and making sure you have a proof of service for each witness. (If you don't have the proof of service, and the witness doesn't show, then you won't have a basis to have the court issue a warrant to have the witness brought to court).

c. Review and discovery of documents, and the subpoenaing of these documents to court.

d. The law permits you to conduct discovery under Local Superior Court Rules and/or the State of California Rules of Court.

In my opinion, this is a step which is not used enough. The social worker's records and files (which are different from the court's records and files) should be obtained and reviewed. There is always the strong possibility that these records and documents will contain information that could assist in your defense.

e. Before the hearing, or trial, you should work on an opening or closing argument with your attorney. These are not always used, and not always required by the court, but it is an excellent way to organize the case for its eventual presentation.

f. Special attention should be given to analyzing the case from the perspective of every participant, the judge, the social worker and her attorney, and the minor's attorneys', etc. Too many times I see clients, and other attorneys, only giving consideration from their own perspective. forgetting that there are sometimes many other competing perspectives in the court room. If these aren't considered, you are not adequately preparing for the trial.

At this point, I must disclose something that is unique to juvenile dependency proceedings. **"Hearsay" evidence is admissible in the social worker's report, but not by the parents.** Yes, this is not a mistake.

It is based on the assumption that the social worker is neutral and objective. An assumption which I have found, in many of my cases, not to be true or accurate.

Many theorize that this assumption is based on simple economics; social workers can't afford the time or resources to prove a child abuse case the old fashioned way; so the courts and legislature have given them this privilege - which in most cases, turns out to be a huge disadvantage for the parents.

The best thing to do is accept this, don't fight it; and work to win your case despite the advantage given the county social worker.

At the trial, the social worker and his/her

attorney must prove, by a "preponderance" of the evidence, that the allegations by the social worker are true. Some legal theorists define the "preponderance" test as "more likely than not" - or more than 50%.

In legal circles, it is believed to be very easy, in most cases. for the social worker to do this. So in order for the parent to win, sometimes extraordinary efforts must be taken to defeat the social worker at this stage of the proceedings.

What Happens at the Trial

1. Typically, the trial starts out by the court asking the County Counsel, the social worker's attorney, if h/she has any documentary evidence to offer into evidence. Most of the time, this consists of the social worker's reports – submitted in the case.
2. The court then asks defense counsel if there is any objection to the reports being admitted into evidence.
3. Then the county counsel calls witnesses. After which, each attorney has a chance to cross-examine the witnesses as they are called.
4. Then the minor's counsel goes through the same steps with documentary evidence and witnesses, and his/her witnesses are cross-examined.

5. Then the parents' attorney goes through the same steps with documentary evidence and witnesses, and his/her witnesses are cross-examined.
6. Then the social worker and her attorney may call "rebuttal" witnesses, to contradict the evidence and the witnesses the parents have presented.
7. After all of this, the attorneys may give the judge closing arguments. Many times, the judge does not want to hear closing arguments, but it's up to each individual judge.
8. I should mention at this point, that the judge may ask questions of any witness during the proceedings.
9. In my opinion, it does make a difference which side the child's attorney comes down on, the parents or the social worker's.
    a. When the minor's attorney is against the parents, time and consideration should be taken as to how the parents' attorney will deal with this situation. The possibilities are almost endless; but they all should be carefully discussed with your attorney

9. The Dispositional Hearing (Dispo, Trial #2)

If the parents lose the adjudication phase, or if they plead at the adjudication phase, the next hearing is the Dispositional Hearing.

This is probably the most important hearing in the entire juvenile dependency process. And, we must remember, if you lose the adjudication trial, this does NOT mean you will lose the dispositional hearing. And, if you win this hearing, the children will be returned to your custody, even though you lost trial #1.

At the dispositional hearing, the social worker must prove by "clear and convincing evidence," that the parents are a "substantial danger" to the children; and that there are no less restrictive alternatives to removing the children from the parents' home.

Many times, I see parents agreeing to "out of home" placement, when they have a good shot at winning the contested dispositional hearing.

I think this happens because many people

act, and believe, that the adjudication and dispositional hearings are one in the same; but they are NOT. They have different legal tests, and different burdens of proof.

1. The first test in the adjudication hearing is the social worker proving you are a "substantial risk" to the children, by the lowest burden of proof - preponderance of evidence.
2. The second test is at the disposition hearing. The social worker must prove that you are a "substantial danger" to the children, by the second highest burden of proof - clear and convincing evidence.
   a. First of all, to be a "substantial danger" to a child, the evidence must prove that you are a bad, really bad, person.
   b. Second, by the time you reach this hearing, most parents have taken classes or counseling to address the problems that originally brought them to the attention of the juvenile court.
   c. Third, clear and convincing evidence is a heightened standard of evidence; and in theory, it should be harder for the social worker to prove.

Many times the adjudication and the disposition hearings are done together, at the same time. And, if that's the case, you must

know this before you lay out your strategy.
1. It will affect the witnesses you may want to bring to court. For example, if the court is going to do both hearings together, you'd want to bring in your instructors and counselors to show how you've remediated the problems which brought you to the court.
2. It will affect the documentary evidence you want to show the judge.

Otherwise, if these hearings are done separately, and sometimes you should request this of the judge, these hearings will be similar to the adjudication hearing mentioned earlier.

Typically, a separate disposition hearing starts out by the court asking the County Counsel, the social worker's attorney, if h/she has any documentation to offer into evidence. Most of the time, this consists of the social worker's reports submitted thus far in the case.

1. The court then asks defense counsel if there is any objection to the reports being admitted into evidence.
2. Then the county counsel calls witnesses, after which, each attorney has a chance to cross-examine the witnesses as they are called.
3. Then the minor's counsel goes through the same steps with documentary

evidence and witnesses, and his/her witnesses are cross examined.
4. Then the parents' attorneys go through the same steps with documentary evidence and witnesses, and his/her witnesses are cross examined.
5. Then the social worker and her attorney may call "rebuttal" witnesses, to contradict what the evidence and the witnesses the parents have presented.
6. After all of this, the attorneys may give the judge closing arguments. Many times, the judge does not want to hear closing arguments, but it's up to each individual judge.

I should mention at this point, that the judge may ask questions of any witness during the proceedings.

Where the minor's attorney is against the parents, time and consideration should be taken as to how parents' attorneys will deal with this situation. The possibilities are almost endless; but it should be carefully discussed with your attorney.

10. The 388 Petition & Hearing

I mentioned this hearing here, because I'd like you to be thinking about this tool all during the juvenile court process. Theoretically, it cannot be used until after the dispositional hearing; therefore, I mention it now.

This is a petition that ANY PERSON can file asking the judge to change a prior court order, and alleging that it would be in the best interests of the children. This petition seems like a somewhat simple form to complete, but its subtleties are complex in most situations.

The typical person using this tool, is a parent who wants the children returned home sooner than the next court hearing. But it's also used by relatives to have children moved from foster care to the relative home. I've seen it used by minors' attorneys and social workers to remove children from a certain placement. I've seen it used by non-relatives to place children in their homes. I've seen it used by parents to stop the termination of their parental rights, and to stop an eventual adoption. The uses are endless, and only limited by the imagination.

If a 388 petition is filed, the court may do one of two things: grant the petition, and set it for a hearing; or deny the petition.

If the petition is denied, you have the right to appeal this decision, immediately.

If the petition is granted, the court can have a hearing on the petition in a variety of ways, all within the discretion of the judge.

The court could set a full evidentiary hearing.

The court could set a hearing where the judge will just listen to oral argument by the attorneys, or any combination thereof.

I once was involved in a 388 petition hearing, where the judge required everyone to submit testimony by written declaration; and then only allowed limited oral argument by the attorneys. This is interesting, because it shows the varieties of ways a 388 hearing can be conducted.

Always consult with an attorney before filing a 388 petition; and always have an attorney represent you in that proceeding. Too many things can happen where legal expertise may be needed.

11. The Sixth Month Review (364, .21E, JR)

Assume you won your case at the dispositional hearing, the case will most likely be continued for a 6 month review pursuant to WIC 364.

During this period of time, a new social worker is assigned to your case; a family maintenance worker. As the name sounds, this social worker's job will be to visit you and your children, at least one time per month, and report your progress back to the court at the end of 6 months.

This worker, if s/he notices any problems, can address the family issues by referring the family to some sort of "family maintenance" service such as counseling or parenting classes.

This family maintenance worker also has the ability to file a new case/petition with the court and remove the children from the parents' custody if s/he believes that the children need protection.

If such a case is filed, the process

mentioned above in earlier chapters just begins again.

The best thing that could probably happen during this period is for the social worker to recommend, at the 6 month review date, that the case be closed. If such is the recommendation, the social worker and the juvenile court is out of your life.

If the social worker does not recommend that the case be closed, you are entitled to have a trial to prove that it should be closed. More specifically, if you have a trial, the social worker has to prove that the case should remain open. These types of cases were not originally designed to go on forever. They were designed to address a family problem, and then close. Ongoing custody and visitation issues should be handled by the Family Law Courts, under the Family Code.

The trial you are entitled to at this point is much like described in earlier chapters, but I will mention it again since it is extremely important for you to be familiar with the concepts of a "trial". (Refer to the process "as described on page 38 – **"What Happens at the Trial"**

    1. Typically, the trial starts out with the court asking the County Counsel, the social worker's attorney, if they have any

documentation to offer into evidence. Most of the time, this consists of the social worker's reports submitted thus far in the case.
2. The court then asks defense counsel if there is any objection to the reports being admitted into evidence.
3. Then the county counsel calls witnesses, after which each attorney has a chance to cross-examine the witnesses, as they are called.
4. Then the minor's counsel goes through the same steps with documentary evidence and witnesses, and his/her witnesses are cross-examined.
5. Then the parents' attorneys go through the same steps with documentary evidence and witnesses, and his/her witnesses are cross-examined.
6. Then the social worker and her attorney may call "rebuttal" witnesses, to contradict the evidence and the witnesses the parents have presented.
7. After all of this, the attorneys may give the judge closing arguments. Many times, the judge does not want to hear closing arguments, but it's up to each individual judge.
8. I should mention at this point that the judge may ask questions of any witness, during the proceedings.
9. Where the minor's attorney is against the parents, time and consideration should be taken as to how the parents' attorney

will deal with this situation. The possibilities are almost endless; but should be carefully discussed with your attorney.

If the case is closed at this point, generally, the court will issue a Family Law Custody and Visitation Order, which is also filed with the Family Law Court in your county. The purpose of this order is to give the parents a starting point for any future custody and visitation disputes.

You are entitled to have a trial or hearing on what this closing order should say and provide. This could be extremely important in the future; and will effect computations of eventual child and/or spousal support.

If an order is issued by the Juvenile Court, any parent can go to the Family Law Court in order to change or modify this order. Generally, there are legal requirements to be met, but that discussion is beyond this book. If you need information, contact a competent Family Law attorney, or contact me. (888) 888-6582.

The second thing which could happen at the six month review is the WIC 366.21(e) hearing. This is the six month hearing that happens if the children weren't returned to your custody at the dispositional hearing.

During this period, you are assigned a social worker called a "Family Reunification" worker (FR Worker). It is supposed to be his/her job to reunify the parents with the children.

However, during this period there is something also happening with the social worker called "Concurrent Planning". This planning consists of the social worker developing a plan for the children to be permanently placed outside your home; in the event you are unable to reunify with them.

You can easily see this Concurrent Planning sometimes clashes with the Family Reunification plan and its goals.

During this period, if the children have not been returned to your custody, it is extremely important for you to:

1. Participate in the FR plan ordered by the judge
2. Take all steps necessary to make sure the children are placed with friendly relatives, even if the relatives are outside the state.
   a. This becomes crucial in subsequent hearings, if the children can't be returned to your home.
3. Make sure you are consistently visiting your children in their out of home

placement. This too will become crucial in subsequent hearings.
4. Make sure you keep in written/email contact with your attorney. It is extremely important that s/he know the progress you are making with the FR plan.
    a. At the actual hearing, if the social worker recommends that the children not be returned to your custody at this time, you are entitled to have a trial at a future date. And, I recommend in most cases, you take advantage of this hearing. My recommendation is based on my experience, but it does vary from case to case.
    b. If you have a trial, it is handled like the trials described above. It is extremely important that you meet and strategize with your attorney.
    c. You will need to subpoena witnesses that will testify on how you have progressed with your FR plan. Their opinions may significantly differ from the opinion of the social worker. Of course, if positive, you'd want the judge to hear this evidence.
    d. The process that follows is a repeat of the steps outlined on pages 22 and 23, **"What Happens at the Trial"**

At the end of the trial the court could do several things:

    i. Adopt the social worker's recommendation not to return the childn at this time
    ii. Return the children, despite the social worker's recommendations
    iii. Liberalize your visitation, from supervised to unsupervised
    iv. Modify your FR case plan
    v. And many other things.

After the hearing, the court may close the case, or continue the case for the WIC 366.21(f) hearing, which is another 6 months down the line.

    i. The exact thing the court is likely to do at this point, like many other things in this process, is determined on the specific facts of your case.
    ii. And, what the court decides at this point, will usually control what you and your attorney should do. But always consult with your attorney, or seek a competent second opinion.

12. The Twelve Month Review Hearing (.21F, PPH)

Assuming the children were not returned at the .21e hearing - this is the 12 month hearing.

During this period, you are still assigned a social worker, (FR Worker). It is supposed to be his/her job to reunify the parents with the children.

During this period "Concurrent Planning" continues, and seems to take on a more important status. The theory being that since you haven't regained custody, it may be unlikely that you may regain custody in the future. This process relates to the social worker developing a plan for the children to be permanently placed outside your home; in the event you are unable to reunify with them.

You can easily see that this Concurrent Planning sometimes clashes with the Family Reunification plan and its goals.

During this period, if the children have not been returned to your custody, it is extremely important for you to continue to participate in the Family Reunification Plan that was ordered by the judge, including consistent visits to your children. You also need to keep in written/email contact with your attorney to keep him/her informed of the progress you are making in the FR plan.

At the actual hearing, if the social worker recommends that the children not be returned to your custody at this time, you are entitled to have a trial at a future date. And, in most cases, I recommend that you take advantage of this hearing. My recommendation is based on my experience, but it does vary from case to case.

If you have a trial, it is handled like the trials described above. It is extremely important that you meet and strategize with your attorney.

You will need to subpoena witnesses that will testify on how you have progressed with your FR plan. Their opinions may significantly differ from the opinion of the social worker. Of course, you'd want the judge to hear this evidence.

At the end of the trial the court could do several things:
1. Adopt the social workers recommendation not to return the children at this time
2. Return the children, despite the social workers recommendations

3. Liberalize your visitation, from supervised to unsupervised
4. Modify you FR case plan
5. Set the case for a hearing pursuant to WIC 366.26 hearing to permanently place your children out of your care.
    a. If this happens, you should confer with your attorney to develop a plan to remedy this situation.
    b. If you cannot accomplish this, you should seek a second opinion from a competent attorney. Time is of the essence, and you should not delay.
    c. There are other appellate remedies which are available, but you must speak to your attorney, because there is a relatively short time period for you to act.

The exact thing the court is likely to do at this point, like many other things in this process, determines on the specifics facts of your case.

And what the court decides at this point, will usually control what you and your attorney should do. But always consult with your attorney, or seek a competent second opinion.

13. The Selection & Implementation Hearing (.26)

If you haven't regained custody of your children by the conclusion of the .21F hearing (Chapter 12), the court will schedule a hearing pursuant to WIC section 366.26. This hearing is supposed to select the best permanent plan for your children.

The first plan the social worker is likely to recommend is adoption by another person/s. Generally, this person is a foster parent, or an unfriendly relative. Adoption means that this person/s becomes the legal parent of your children; and that you and your family have no further rights or interests in the children. You lose the children forever.

When a relative adopts the children, that relative becomes the parent. For example, if your parents adopt the children, they become the parents of the children and you are not a brother or sister of the children. But if your in-laws adopt the children, you are of no relationship to the children.

Either way, you have no rights to visitation with the children, and if you are to see the children in the future, that will be at the sole discretion of the new adoptive parents.

Unless you were to win an appeal, an adoption cannot be overturned.

I am aware that it may be theoretically possible to bring a lawsuit to overturn an adoption, but it is highly unlikely.

The second plan that the social worker may recommend is legal guardianship. Under this plan, you remain the parent; but the legal guardian becomes the permanent care taker of the child, until age 18; making all the decisions about the child. You may have the right to visit; most likely these will be supervised or monitored visits.

You may have the right to overturn the legal guardianship and regain custody of the children. You need to discuss this option with a competent attorney.

The third plan the social worker may recommend is Long Term Foster care. Under this plan, the child remains with the foster parent, relative or family friend until the child is 18 years of age. This plan is rarely used these days. In most cases, social workers and courts opt for the more "favored" plan of permanency, which is adoption.

To prepare for the contested .26 hearing:

The first hearing will be to inform the judge if you agree or disagree with the social worker's recommendations. If you don't agree, the court will set a trial/contest date for you to challenge the social worker's recommendations.

If the recommendation is for adoption, you will immediately want to sit and discuss the case, and your alternatives, with your attorney. Needless to say, permanently losing your children is an extremely important topic, and you need to know what can be done to stop or delay this from happening.

A. 388 petition (See Chapter 10)

One of the first things I recommend is that the parent/s file a 388 petition and ask for several different remedies. Most of the time, I request return of the child, further Family Reunification Services, additional visitation to increase the bond between the parent and children, or placement of the children with friendly relatives.

The strategies and steps to implement some or all of these alternatives are beyond the scope of this book. Suffice it to say, you should discuss these things with your attorney, and if s/he is not willing to go through this process, you may want to consider changing attorneys.

B. Bonding Study

A "bonding study" between you and the children is extremely important. You should request that your attorney arrange such a study with a local expert; and in some cases the court may be willing to pay for it pursuant to Evidence Code section 730. If not, you may have to cover that cost.

During this time frame, it becomes important that you have continuous and frequent visitation. This, and other things that may help you stop or delay the termination of your parental rights, will most likely be fought by the social worker, the social worker's attorney, and in a lot of cases, by the children's attorney.

So you can see the importance in making sure your attorney takes the time and interest in implementing a plan to save your parental rights.

C. Notice of Appeal

If you lose this hearing, you should

immediately ask your attorney to file the Notice of Appeal form. It is a two page form. If s/he is unable to do that for you, you have 60 days in which to file that form. The only hope that you may have to regain custody, or to prevent an adoption, is by way of this appeal.

If you cannot afford an appellate attorney, the appellate court will provide one for you; or you may hire your own.

Note that your appeal will only be based on the evidence submitted in the trial court. So, it is important that you and your attorney meet and confer in advance to determine the witnesses and documentary evidence that is going to be submitted to the court at this hearing.

Most important, is the subpoenaing of certain witnesses, to ensure their presence. If a witness is not present, it is unlikely the judge will give you a continuance to bring in that witness, unless you have a proof of service that the witness was served, but did not show.

Please call me for a free consultation regarding your .26 hearing, or the appeal from your .26 hearing, or the denial of your 388 petition.
(888) 888-6582.

14. Foster Parents Rights

Foster Parents may have certain rights in the relationship, custody and visitation of a foster child. They may not have the same rights that a parent has, or a relative. But they do indeed have rights. Many times I'm confronted with foster parents who have been told by a county social worker that they do not have rights, and that is simply not true.

Generally, the foster parent may be losing the foster child, because the social worker has decided to move the child to another foster home. This may be able to be stopped.

Or, the foster parent may be losing the child, because the social worker has decided to move the child to a blood relative. This may be able to be stopped.

Or, the foster parent may be losing the child, because the social worker has decided to return the child to a parent.

The key things that the foster parent must file are:

1. De Facto Motion
2. 388 petition
3. 827 petition
4. Petitions for legal guardianship, both temporary and permanent.

But it should be noted that the filing of these documents is about 40 percent of the work; and not even the most important part. The most important part for this to be successful is the representation you receive at the hearings or mini trials for these proceedings.

Sometimes, concurrently with this, the State of California initiates administrative court proceedings to discipline a foster parent, or to revoke the foster parents' license or certification. These proceedings are not in the Juvenile Court, but in the Office of Administrative Hearings, located around the state.

These hearings are special administrative hearings, and are usually prosecuted by the State Attorney General's Office, and/or the State Community Licensing Department's Legal Department. I recommend that you not try to represent yourself; there are special rules of procedure and evidence which can apply to these proceedings.

Please call me for a free consultation regarding your foster care situation. (888) 888-6582.

15. The Secret

Everything that I've written in previous chapters in this book is significant information and critical to winning your case. In fact, everything I've written in these chapters could be considered a "secret." However, I'd like to share with you an additional comment that I consider of special relevance to every Juvenile Dependency (CPS) case.

When I was a child, I practiced an ancient Japanese martial art, Judo. Judo actually means "the gentle way", yet one of the secrets to Judo, among other things, was to keep your opponent close. If you held your opponent close, you were more likely to be able to flip and pin the opponent to the floor. On the same note, Machiavelli wrote in the famous 15th Century book, The Prince, "keep your friends close, but your enemy's closer."

The same advice is true in most legal cases; including juvenile dependency cases and cases involving Child Protective Services ("CPS") or Department of Children and Family Services ("DCFS"). Many people focus on the facts that their rights have been violated, and not enough focus is given to working on getting the children back into their custody.

I often ask clients,

"Do you want to be right, or do you want to get your children back."

I know that you may be feeling that this whole process is an "injustice" and that your rights have been trampled on – and possibly violated. But, in most cases, it's not possible to vindicate your rights while at the same time winning the case in order to regain custody of your children.

If you want you want to go after the social worker and the county, save that fight for the subsequent lawsuit in Federal Court for civil rights violations. The juvenile judge may not be interested in the fact that your civil rights were violated, and the fact that they were, will not help you win the juvenile case.

I know that this may be a hard pill to swallow, but in my almost 30 years of experience, it is an unfortunate truth.

Here's an example of a case that I was involved in recently that illustrates this concept even further:

A young mother had been involved (for a couple of years) in Juvenile Dependency Court -

with several court-appointed attorneys – and she was increasingly frustrated with the system and the social workers, yet desperate to get her child back. She felt the social workers' requests were unreasonable, frivolous, and things were being asked of her that she deemed unnecessary to the case.

Her reactions to these requests may have been easily interpreted by judges, social workers and other administrators involved in the case as obstinate and/or combative – perhaps she was perceived as being uncooperative, impulsive, acting out aggressively, or displaying anger management issues. Even though this was not the case, she was having a difficult time convincing others that she was "fit" to get her children back.

She finally hired my firm to represent her. After we appeared in court with her the first time, she was upset – and tearful – that the attorney assigned to the case seemed to be agreeing to these "frivolous" requests. This led her to the belief that everyone was against her, and that we weren't fighting for her rights.

We talked. I gently reminded her of my mantra:

"Do you want to be right, or do you want to get your children back."

After a lengthy discussion, she agreed to do her best and comply fully with the social workers' requests, and - as we anticipated - at the next court hearing, her case was dismissed.

So, now you know my secret – and it can be yours, too. As in the ancient martial art of judo ("the gentle way") study your "opponent". Draw him or her close – master and control the situation. Don't get "out of control." Realize that resistance can be perceived as a barrier or roadblock – making the requests/demands of the social workers even more difficult to overcome.

As in all life situations, there's a hard and expensive way to do things, and there's an easier and less expensive ("gentle way") to do things. The ultimate goal is to win. The choice is yours, I can do both.

Made in the USA
San Bernardino, CA
08 June 2016